Listening Hearts:

Manual for Discussion Leaders

MOREHOUSE PUBLISHING

Listening Hearts

Manual for Discussion Leaders

Suzanne Farnham
Edward Holm
Sherry Kolbe
Louise Miller
Peggy McLean
Taylor McLean
Edward Mortimore
Billie Stewart
Richard Weise

Morehouse Publishing
P.O. Box 1321
Harrisburg, PA 17105

Library of Congress Cataloging-in-Publication Data
Listening hearts : manual for discussion leaders / Suzanne Farnham ... [et al.]
    p.   cm.
    Includes bibliographical reference.
    ISBN 0-8192-1608-9
    1. Vocation.   2. Discernment of spirits.   3. Christian communities.   4. Spiritual life—Anglican Communion.   I. Farnham, Suzanne G.
BV4740.L57   1991 Suppl.   93-23425
253—dc20   CIP

Printed in the United States of America

Second Printing, 1997

CONTENTS

ACKNOWLEDGMENTS

Nine people associated with the discernment program of what was then the Christian Vocation Project worked in community to write this manual. They began each meeting with a time of silence and worked together toward Quaker consensus. They wrote a preliminary draft, then field-tested and refined it, drawing upon real-life experiences.

Supporting their efforts were many other people. Most especially, Marilynn Cornejo and Adele Free provided secretarial and administrative assistance, John McIntyre edited the copy, and Chris Hotvedt did the design work.

Another group of people led discussions to field-test the manual: Paul Beares, Susan Beares, Suzanne Farnham, Adele Free, Edward Holm, Stephanie Hull, Sherry Kolbe, Margie Lance, Louise E. Miller, Peggy McLean, Taylor McLean, Edward Mortimore, Fred Ruof, and Jeannine Ruof.

The Christian Vocation Project, now known as Listening Hearts Ministries, began in Baltimore as a ministry of Memorial Episcopal Church, which has provided continual support. Funding has come from private contributors across the country as well as from Memorial Episcopal Church, the Episcopal Church Foundation, and the Diocese of Maryland, where it is a CROSS+ROADS Program. More than a hundred fifty people have volunteered their services, including a number who have offered their professional services *pro bono*.

May joyful thanks abound for the dedication of so many people who have made this manual possible.

INTRODUCTION

This *Manual for Discussion Leaders* provides ideas and suggestions for people who will be leading discussions on the book *Listening Hearts*, to help them draw up plans tailored to their own groups. It can be used to design a single session as well as a course that lasts a number of sessions. The leadership can be provided by one person, or shared by two or more.

Listening Hearts explores the relationships among call, discernment, and community. It is brimming with sentences that can evoke thoughtful discussion. The quality of the discussion will be enhanced if those present have read the book, marked and reflected on the parts that catch their attention, and brought the book with them. Perhaps the most important thing a leader can do is to make every effort to get the participants to read and mark the book beforehand.

PURPOSES OF
DISCUSSION PROGRAM

- To help participants clarify and expand their understanding of call, ministry, discernment, and community as they relate to one another.

- To provide participants an opportunity to grow in their relationship with God.

- To increase a sense of listening to God in themselves, through others, and in everyday occurrences.

- To enable participants to become more aware of the value of the support of a faith community.

Leaders are invited to consider what they would like to accomplish through the discussions, modifying the above purposes if they wish.

III

PREPARING FOR A
DISCUSSION SERIES

All parties — Listening Hearts Ministries, the leader, and the participants — have roles in a discussion series.

- <u>Listening Hearts Ministries</u> has developed the resources — *Listening Hearts* and this *Manual for Discussion Leaders*. Leaders should feel free to call the office of Listening Hearts Ministries (410-225-9054) with any questions or concerns.

- The <u>discussion leader</u> plans the sessions, structures the environment, and facilitates the discussions. Discussion leaders need to read and reread the entire book — including the appendices, endnotes, and annotated bibliography.

- The <u>participants</u> need to **read** *Listening Hearts* and **reflect** on the material prior to the meeting, to **attend** regularly, to **listen** to others in the group, and to **share** their own ideas. It will help if leaders convey this to the group.

A CHECKLIST:

1. Read this *Manual for Discussion Leaders*.

2. Read *Listening Hearts*.

3. Confer with the appropriate people about the general plan (for instance, it might be a five-week Sunday adult forum series or a study group committed to regular attendance at two-hour sessions for eight consecutive meetings). Set the dates and times.

4. Develop a framework for the series. Because the initial session uses considerable time for introductory purposes, it may be a good idea to plan to spend additional time with Chapter One at the beginning of the second session.

5. Plan the publicity. Recruit people to carry out the publicity plan. Ask clergy to express support in their Sunday announcements. Some additional possibilities: (a) a newsletter article two months ahead of time; (b) a follow-up article a month ahead; (c) fliers inserted in the Sunday bulletin as the event draws near; (d) brief weekly reminders in the Sunday bulletin; (e) posters strategically placed about the premises.

6. Select the space. A quiet, comfortable room — free of interruptions — is best.

7. In the publicity, stress the importance of reading the book, marking the parts that particularly resonate, and bringing the book to the discussions. Encourage participants to attend all of the sessions.

8. Make an all-out campaign to distribute *Listening Hearts* well in advance of the discussion series.

9. If the participants are expected to sign up ahead of time, you may want to ask them to write down their hopes for the series as part of the registration. Review the responses carefully; keep the information in mind as you prepare for the discussions.

10. Perhaps provide a list of the participants' names, addresses, and phone numbers to distribute to each member of the group.

11. Re-read *Listening Hearts* carefully, including the appendices, endnotes, and annotated bibliography. Highlight and make notations in the book.

12. Assemble any supplies that you might want for the series, such as paper and pencils. Make copies of the feedback form, using the master copy provided in this book. It is helpful to have extra copies of *Listening Hearts* available at the discussions in case some people arrive without them.

13. If the sessions will exceed an hour and a half in length, a short break may be advisable.

It is impossible to discuss the entire book in one session. If a single discussion is planned instead of a series, it is best to limit the discussion to one chapter, or at the most one section (call, discernment, or community). The discussion will be more coherent if the scope is limited. Unless a group is well grounded in the material, it is preferable to start at the beginning of the book, since each chapter builds on what precedes it.

If planning an extended in-depth study, the leader may want to devote more than one session to most chapters, having the group take time to delve into the endnotes and related appendices. Readings from the books in the annotated bibliography will further enrich the discussions.

STRUCTURING THE DISCUSSION SESSION

*L*istening Hearts seeks to touch people's experiences. A good discussion will provide participants with opportunities to identify significant life experiences, reflect on how God may have been acting in those experiences, and consider where the Spirit may be pointing through them. A purely intellectual or theoretical discussion can block such personal reflection.

Leaders can encourage reflective dialogue by saying a few words about the concept at the beginning of each session and then offering reminders if needed. Leaders will also do well to suggest that participants listen carefully and prayerfully to one another, not interrupt each other, and allow a few moments of silence between speakers (wait-time). This will give the group time to absorb what is said and permit the speaker the opportunity to continue on to express a deeper thought should one be forming beneath the surface.

Since the intent of the discussion is to encourage reflection, there is no need to cover all the material in a chapter. Instead of focusing on the content of the book, **use the content of the book to focus on God's actions in the lives of those present.**

The leader will need to develop a plan for each session. It will include plans for opening and closing the session, along with strategies to enable those in the group to listen to one another in an attempt to hear God and look for the movement of the Holy Spirit in the events of their lives.

THE INITIAL SESSION

In the initial session of a series, some preliminaries need to be covered:
- Introduction of leaders
- Introduction of group
- Overview of series

Introduction of Leaders

Leaders begin to set the tone for the series during the introductions. If they introduce themselves to the group by saying something about how God has guided their lives and what the book means to them personally, and if they can do this in a relaxed and open way, they set an example for the group. Groups feel more comfortable with leaders who convey a sense of who they are.

If the individual sessions are short (an hour or less), introductions will need to be brief. With longer sessions, the leaders can take a little more time to introduce themselves.

Introduction of Group

Unless the leaders and the members of the group all know each other, it is important to give the members an opportunity to introduce themselves in some way that ties in with the subject matter.

If the group is small, the leader might invite those present to give their names and say something about what brings them to this discussion program.

If the group is large, and there is not time for individual introductions, the best way to provide this opportunity may be to ask the group a few questions such as:

- Do you all have copies of *Listening Hearts*?
- How thoroughly have you read the book?
- Were the ideas in the book new to you?

OVERVIEW OF THE SERIES

Leaders need to set the stage for the series by:

- Stating how many sessions are planned
- Indicating which chapters will be covered in the series
- Presenting the purposes of the discussion program
- Discussing the responsibilities of the participants (attendance, preparation, listening, "wait-time," sharing)
- Asking the group to speak from their own experience and to avoid being abstract or hypothetical.

Design For Each Session

If leaders are scheduled to lead a session and were not present at the previous session, it is essential that they get a thorough briefing from the person(s) who led the previous session as far in advance as possible.

Opening the Session

- If anyone, leader or participant, is new to the group, provide for appropriate introductions.
- A prayer or a short time of silence may help center the group in God.
- Specify which chapter is the focus for this session.
- Plan some words of transition to bridge the previous discussion and the current one. This could be done by asking the group what portions of the previous week's discussion meant the most to them.

Conducting the Discussion

Try to let the group establish the direction of the discussion within the limits of the designated chapter. The best discussions are likely to emerge from material that has caught the interest of those present.

- Begin by asking the group to open their books to the appointed chapter.
- Inquire if anyone was drawn to a particular passage. Ask each person who responds to cite the page; then invite the group to locate the passage in their own books. This often draws participants into discussion as they pick up on nuances and various facets of meaning within the passage.
- When someone identifies a passage to look at, invite that person to say something about his or her own experience in relation to it.
- Then invite others in the group to consider their experiences in relation to the selected passage.
- Try to make sure that everyone who wants to speak about a given passage has an opportunity to do so before moving on to another place.
- Continue to invite the members to select portions they want to discuss until they have covered all the segments that drew

their attention. This may well occupy the
entire session.

- When the group has no further points to
  bring up for discussion, the leaders can
  introduce various passages they have
  marked in their own books.
- If time remains, suggested questions for the
  chapter found in this manual may be used.
- If the group is too large to permit full
  participation by each person present, the
  group may be sub-divided into groups of
  three or four for a portion of the session.

CLOSING THE DISCUSSION

- A few minutes before it is time to end,
  leaders should announce that it is time to
  conclude the discussion.
- Leaders may offer a few reflective thoughts
  about the discussion, but it is best not to try
  to pull everything into a neat package. It
  may be appropriate to mention that the
  most important thing a discussion such as
  this can accomplish is to quicken the
  movement of the Spirit within those present
  and raise new questions for the group to
  ponder.

- Leaders should announce the plans for the next session. At the final session of the series, they can tell the group about some of the other offerings of Listening Hearts Ministries: the *Listening Hearts* series of books, retreats on *Listening Hearts*, workshops for approaching group decisions through discernment, and training for discerners in order to set up a discernment program for the congregation.

- A good way to end each discussion session is to offer the Thomas Merton prayer at the end of *Listening Hearts*. It can be read by one member of the group or corporately either silently or aloud. Leaders may want to invite the members to form a circle and join hands.

FEEDBACK FORMS

A master copy of the feedback form is provided at the end of this manual. Allow time at the end of the final session for participants to fill out the forms.

SUGGESTIONS FOR LEADING DISCUSSIONS

The following are some specific suggestions for the discussion leader:

FACILITATING THE GROUP

- Arrange the chairs in a circle.
- Open the discussion series with informal introductions.
- Keep the discussion on track. Try to limit your own participation either to areas that are overlooked or are confusing and need clarification.
- Take time every once in a while to draw loose ends together.
- Encourage sharing of insights so that participants can benefit from one another's experiences.
- Provide people with the opportunity to respond to the discussion before moving on.

("Would anyone else like to say anything about this?")

- Help the group to follow the thread. ("Has anyone else had a similar experience?")
- Give less assertive people a chance to participate. ("Would anyone who has not yet spoken like to say anything?")
- If someone introduces an issue that more appropriately belongs to a chapter scheduled for another session, intervene and point out that the subject relates to a different chapter.
- If someone gets off the topic for the session and onto one not scheduled for another time, intervene and suggest that the group might schedule a separate discussion on that subject at a future date.
- Express satisfaction with the discussion and end on a positive note.

ASKING QUESTIONS

- Follow the flow of the discussion. Use questions to draw out quiet individuals, broaden the discussion beyond a few vocal participants, explore varying viewpoints, and focus the discussion on the topic assigned for the day.

- Keep your questions friendly and sincere so that participants sense that you are trying to be helpful. ("How do *you* see that point?" "How did that work for you?" "How else might this be viewed?")
- Give participants time to respond. Pause after a question to allow time for reflection.
- To encourage careful listening, do not routinely repeat your question or the participant's response.
- Ask participants for clarification as needed.
- When a participant addresses a question to the leader, the leader can increase participation by asking if anyone in the group would like to respond.

PROBLEM AREAS

- If a member of the group tends to dominate or disrupt the discussion, be polite but try to provide opportunities for others to talk. Comments such as this may help the group to move on: "Thanks. Your comments have been very helpful. Does anyone else have something to say about that point?"
- If members of the group are hesitant to join in the discussion, it is beneficial to provide opportunities for them to speak if they wish,

but also to realize that some people may prefer to remain silent.

- If people begin to intellectualize, draw them back to personal experiences.
- If one person is critical of another's view, suggest to the group that it is preferable to speak of one's own experiences and avoid taking issue with each other.

SUGGESTED QUESTIONS

articipants are expected to read *Listening Hearts* before the discussion. Typically, they will have ideas and questions of their own about the reading and will be prepared to discuss the content. However, the following questions may be useful in stimulating the discussion or moving it back to the topic if the discussion wanders. Leaders are encouraged to select the particular questions that seem best suited to their particular group.

If people respond to questions with a simple "yes" or "no," leaders can invite them to say more, or else follow up with questions such as "Why?" or "How?"

CHAPTER 1:
WHAT IS "CALL" FOR THE CHRISTIAN?

- Have you had a sense of "call" in your life?
- How is a call "to be" different from a call "to do"?

- What do you consider your primary work?
- Do you ever hear God in silence?
- Do you hear God speaking through art?
  dance? nature? literature? music? your
  senses? your imagination? your dreams? your
  pain? pleasure? people? events?
- Does God reach you through Scripture?
  liturgy? communion? community?
- Are there other ways God communicates
  with you?
- Do you ever resist listening for God's call?
- If you heard God's call clearly, would you be
  willing to follow it no matter what God was
  asking?
- When God asks you to do something, have
  you found that God also gives you what you
  need to carry it out? When do you receive
  this grace or strength or help?

CHAPTER 2:
CALL TO MINISTRY

- What is the difference between doing good
  and following a call to ministry?
- How can human motivations for doing
  service hinder our response to God's call?
  Do we have to wait until our motivations
  are pure before responding? How important
  is it for us to be aware of our mixed
  motivations?

- Have you experienced ministry in your life? (ministry through others? ministry through yourself?)

CHAPTER 3:
WHAT IS DISCERNMENT?

- Have you made any conscious efforts to discern God's voice in your life? How have you gone about it? How has it worked out? Did it affect your relationship with God?
- How can voices that are good in and of themselves drown out the voice of God?
- How can identifying your gifts help you with discernment? How might over-emphasizing identification of gifts inhibit discernment?
- Why is discernment partial, tentative, seldom certain?
- How could making discernment a goal undermine discernment?

CHAPTER 4:
WHAT CONDITIONS HELP DISCERN GOD'S CALL?

- What practices or attitudes have helped to open your eyes, ears, and heart to God's voice?

- What roadblocks have kept you from truly seeking God's guidance?
- What things in your life cause anxiety or resistance when you are confronted with a call from God?
- Is there a difference between listening and hearing? Between hearing and obeying?
- What is the purpose of silence? Are there different kinds of silence? What does silence have to do with hearing God?
- Have you heard God through your pain? pleasure? emotions? senses?
- What does "listening with every fiber of your being" mean to you?
- Do you ever experience God through what you do not want to hear?
- How important is it for you to set aside time for prayer, reading, contemplation, listening? Do you set aside the time? What effect does this have?
- Do you ever feel a need to be less somber in your prayer?
- How much do you trust God to lead you? How much confidence do you have in God's guidance? How has your own experience influenced your ability to trust God?
- Do you ever experience God's presence through Scripture?
- What does the word "humility" mean to you?
- Can humility be gained by seeking it directly?

- Does being close to God make us humble? Does being humble bring us closer to God?
- How can our human timetables interfere with hearing God's call?
- What problems can arise from feeling too pressured to hear God's voice? What problems can arise from exercising too much patience? How do we know what is too much?
- Have you ever turned to God for help? What happened?
- Have events in your own life led you to hear God or experience God?
- What is prayer for you? What is your practice?
- To what extent is reading Scripture part of your life?
- Do you feel a tension between being patient and having a sense of urgency?

CHAPTER 5: IS IT GOD WE ARE HEARING?

- Has God's way of communicating with you changed over the years? If so, can you see any pattern in the change?
- As you look back on your life, are there turning points where you can now see that God was at work? If so, can you envision them as arrows pointing the way?

- Can you think of an occasion on which you made a decision in response to what you believed to be God's call? As you lived out your decision, did you get any confirmation of the call? Any refinement? Any re-direction?
- Has one call ever led to another for you?
- What might it mean if some signs of God's call are present but others are not?
- Have threads of your life that seemed unrelated ever converged? If so, how did you feel? Did you discover new meaning for your life? Did the discovery produce any momentum?
- Do you sometimes yearn to be called to something big, important, or glamorous? Are you ever tempted to avoid finding a call in the small things right where you are?
- Do you sense yourself as having a unique combination of qualities that make you who you are and distinguish you from all other people? If so, does that suggest that God may have a unique purpose for you?
- Do you feel that God ever put you in a position beyond your ability to handle and then gave you what you needed to handle it?
- Can you see connections in your life between burn-out and (a) trying to do more than you were supposed to be doing? or (b) being on the wrong track altogether?

- Do you think that you have ever done the right thing at the wrong time? If so, would closer attention to God's guidance have enabled you to act at the right time?
- Do you think that what is apparently the right thing for you to do must be the right thing for others to do as well?
- When seeking God's guidance, do you turn to Scripture for help? If so, how do you go about it and how does it help?
- Do moral codes such as the Ten Commandments help you? How do you avoid rationalizing the way in which they apply to your circumstances? How do you apply moral codes to your life? When do you have difficulty applying them?
- Do you have any experience that helps you to understand what the term "false peace" means? Have you had any vivid experience of an authentic peace?
- Can you think of any examples in your own life journey in which you felt disoriented but then moved into a feeling of calm and serenity?

Chapter 6: Why is Christian Community Important in Discerning God's Call?

- What is a faith community? Do you have more than one?
- Has a faith community ever helped you to hear or follow God's call to you? Has a faith community ever hindered you in this?
- Can involvement with a faith community make it easier to live out your call? Can it be difficult to live out your call without the support of a faith community?
- Have you experienced God's presence in Christian community?

Chapter 7: The Value of a Discernment Group

- Can you think of any advantages of using a group for discernment instead of the help of only one other person?
- Why use a discernment group instead of simply discussing an issue with a group of friends?
- Have you been in a group in which consensus was used rather than majority rule for decisions? Was there a difference in the dynamics? How did you feel as a participant?

- What is the difference between Quaker consensus and consensus as practiced in secular groups?
- What conditions are conducive to reaching consensus?
- "The silence of prayerful listening is not so much the absence of talk as it is presence to the Word." Can you relate this idea to discernment?
- Why is prayerful silence essential to a discernment group?

Chapter 8: Supporting the Ministries of Others

- How do you see yourself as giving, as well as receiving, support?
- What kinds of support do you look for?
- What are the dangers of not having support?
- Do you see a distinction between supporting a person and supporting that person's ministry?
- Do you think it is difficult to keep a support group centered in Christ? What precautions might help?
- If your ministry is outside the church, are there reasons to have it connected with a community of faith?

Chapter 9:
Accountability for
Ministries

- What feelings does the word "accountability" elicit in you? To whom do you feel accountable?
- Do you feel any inner resistance to the idea that you are accountable to others?
- Do you find it difficult to maintain a Christ-like spirit as you get involved in the work of ministry? If so, what is the source of these difficulties? Do you see how a ministry support group might help you?
- Has your being accountable to others ever seemed to make people more willing to support your ministry?
- Has your accountability to others ever seemed to strengthen the quality of ministry?
- To what extent do you see your response to call as a shared responsibility with your Christian community?

LISTENING HEARTS
AND LISTENING HEARTS
MINISTRIES

*L*istening Hearts is the foundation for the activities of Listening Hearts Ministries, which includes discernment programs, with training for leaders; retreats and workshops; and a newsletter entitled *Explorations.* It is also the seminal work for the *Listening Hearts* series of books, including this manual, *Listening Hearts Retreat Designs and Meditation Exercises, The Listening Hearts Songbook,* and *Grounded in God: Listening Hearts Discernment for Group Deliberations.* A discussion series is a good way to prepare a group for these programs and materials as well as introducing them to the book.

Both the book and the project came into being through one woman's commitment to discerning her call and living it out. Becoming acquainted with the Quaker approach to group discernment and aware of the depth of wisdom embedded in other Christian traditions, she sensed the richness possible if all of these strands could be pulled together. She recruited over fifty people to do research and from that group formed a smaller group who worked together for two and a half years to sift through the information and develop a discernment program. The *Listening Hearts* series of books and Listening Hearts Ministries are fruits of that effort.

Further information is available from Listening Hearts Ministries, 1407 Bolton Street, Baltimore, Maryland 21217-4202, telephone 410-225-9054, fax 410-225-3695, e-mail: listen@erols.com.

FEEDBACK

FEEDBACK FORM:
LISTENING HEARTS DISCUSSION SERIES

While the following questions might be answered with a simple "yes" or "no," please elaborate where appropriate.

1. Did these discussions give you an opportunity to grow in your relationship with God?

2. Do you feel that you have developed a stronger awareness of listening to God in yourself?

3. Do you feel that you have developed a stronger awareness of listening to God in others?

4. To what extent did you read *Listening Hearts* in preparation for these discussions?

5. How many sessions did you attend?

6. Do you have additional comments?